APPARITIONS

DEDICATED TO LIBRARIANS EVERYWHERE

APPARITIONS

Architecture That Has Disappeared From Our Cities

T. John Hughes

Published in Australia in 2015 by
The Images Publishing Group Pty Ltd
ABN 89 059 734 431
6 Bastow Place, Mulgrave, Victoria 3170, Australia
Tel: +61 3 9561 5544 Fax: +61 3 9561 4860
books@imagespublishing.com
www.imagespublishing.com
Author contact: tjohnhughes1@gmail.com

National Library of Australia Cataloguing-in-Publication entry:

Title: Apparitions : architecture that has disappeared from our cities
Author: Hughes, T. John, author.
ISBN: 9781864705959 (hardback)
Subjects: Architecture—United States—Pictorial works.
                Historic buildings—United States—Pictorial works.
                Historic preservation—United States.
                Streetscapes (urban design)—United States—Pictorial works.
Dewey Number: 779.473

Coordinating Editor: Sabita Naheswaran

Designed by Ryan Marshall, The Graphic Image Studio Pty Ltd, Mulgrave, Australia
www.tgis.com.au

Pre-publishing services by United Graphic Pte Ltd, Singapore
Printed by Everbest Printing Co. Ltd., in Hong Kong/China

IMAGES has included on its website a page for special notices in relation to this and our other publications.
Please visit www.imagespublishing.com.

CONTENTS

At one time I worked for a social action program whose

offices were headquartered in one-half of a decidedly

unglamorous motel. When the program ended the motel was

replaced by a handsome high-rise. Years later I regularly passed

by this location and often thought about the motel and colorful staff

that were metaphorically ghosted inside the new building.

This is the how Apparitions *began.*

BOSTON

The Head House, designed by Boston's official architect E. M. Wheelwright, was a bathhouse with changing rooms, cafes, and "retiring rooms" for men and women. Completed in 1895, its style was influenced by the German pavilion at the World's Columbian Exposition (the legendary "White City" world's fair) in Chicago.

It was damaged but still standing following the Great New England Hurricane of 1938, a storm so powerful its peak gust of 186mph is the highest hurricane wind ever recorded in the U.S.

Finally, a major fire in 1942 led to its demolition.

LOS ANGELES

The elaborate Richfield Building, with a tower on top and a luxurious Art Deco and Style Moderne lobby, exemplified the temples of commerce built between 1900 and 1930. Its black and gold exterior paid homage to "black gold", as oil was once nicknamed. Its ghosted image almost seems to be reflected in one of the two Modernist towers that replaced it in 1970.

The loss of this downtown landmark helped galvanize the Los Angeles preservation movement.

DETROIT

An elaborate City Hall constructed using expensive materials and boasting a prominent bell tower / observation deck, stood in downtown Detroit from 1870 to 1961. Its eclectic style combined French Second Empire with Italian Renaissance. Of its numerous sculptures, the grandest represented early French explorers such as Cadillac and LaSalle.

By 1950, two large organizations battled over the building's fate. Debate raged around classic issues such as the value of presenting a progressive city image versus respecting history. Eventually the dominant mid-twentieth century view of progress triumphed—out with the old and in with the new.

AUSTIN

This quotation is from the Historic American Building Survey in the 1930s: *"As the surrounding city has changed during the twentieth century, the Houghton House has remained one of the major historical and architectural symbols reflecting life in Austin in the late nineteenth century."*

After a long, contentious debate, it was demolished in favor of a parking garage in 1973.

SAN ANTONIO

In a sense, one icon has replaced another on this block. Sears, an all-purpose department store and mail order firm, was familiar to everyone in the U.S. during the 20th century.

Ricardo Legorreta (1931–2011), the most famous Mexican architect of his generation, was known to all within the world of architecture. Influenced by Luis Barragán and his Mexican roots, Legorreta worked more outside his country than in it. His bold, colorful geometric forms seem to grab the viewer's attention, and are epitomized by the San Antonio Central Library.

Interestingly, the number of books checked out doubled the first year it opened.

ORLANDO

A notable landmark, Wigwam Village offered unique lodging for travelers in the West and South. Shaped like Native American teepees, but containing modern conveniences, these were quirky examples of highway Americana. Developer Frank Redford's inspiration is said to have been a visit to the Great Sioux Reservation, and seeing an ice cream stand with a giant upside down cone.

Today, a more generic motel stands on the site.

PORTLAND, OREGON

Cast iron was a very popular facade in this city; from 1850 to 1890 around 90% of new buildings employed it. Cast iron allowed for a great variety of decorative styles, a decrease in cost, and an increase in the speed of construction. However, claims of its fire resistance proved incorrect and many were lost in the citywide blaze of 1873.

Later, changing tastes and highway projects like this one on Front Street took their toll. What remains is a mixture of renovated, reworked, and lost structures.

BALTIMORE

During the 1960s, grand private residences, like this one owned by Marie Bauernschmidt, were often replaced by multi-unit high rises. The wealthy were moving from the core cities, the economic value of their residences decreased, and the preservation movement had yet to gain significant traction. Subsequently, simple economics guided decisions to demolish mansions all around the country.

Mrs. Bauernschmidt, a health and education activist, was a lifelong Democrat, but a sharp critic of both parties. Prior to elections, she would buy radio time to broadcast her personal opinions of the candidates.

NEW YORK

The Singer Building, headquarters for the Singer sewing machine company, was purposely designed to draw attention to itself. The original ten floors covered most of a city block, and the addition of an elegant, slender tower made it the tallest building in the world (for one year, at least).

The detailed interior and exterior design by French-trained architect Ernest Flagg succeeded in attracting attention. However, the floor plan was not practical for U.S. Steel, who bought the building and demolished it in 1968. A "glass box" with five times as much square footage replaced it.

SACRAMENTO

Before railroads the West Coast was very isolated from the economic centers of the East Coast. In 1863, financial heavyweights including Mark Hopkins, Charles Crocker, and Leland Stanford (former governor and future university founder) formed the Central Pacific Railroad. The railroad's depot is shown here.

They oversaw the construction of the track eastward and, in 1869, east and west work crews met at famed Promontory Point, Utah.

In 1926, the depot was demolished. With the dramatic changes to modes of transportation in the 20th Century, railroad usage severely declined, and train yards have become unused or repurposed areas.

MADISON, WISCONSIN

A relatively unknown project by an extremely well-known architect is the boathouse on Lake Mendota designed by Frank Lloyd Wright. Having lived in Madison for much of his young life, Wright knew the area well. In 1893, at the age of 26, he won a competition to create this softly curved structure as well as another boathouse on Lake Monona. An economic downturn and some citizen complaints scuttled the second project.

And in 1928, for reasons that are not particularly clear, the Mendota municipal boathouse was demolished.

SAN FRANCISCO

Two firehouses, completely different in appearance, have occupied this address. One, built in 1884, was a Gothic Revival style structure that signified a return to romantic, pre-industrial sensibilities. With its towers, steep roofs, and porches, this style was used in homes as well as high-profile structures like New York's St. Patrick's cathedral. The no nonsense 1960s design of its replacement seems to be much more grounded in function than fashion.

Although the pump wagon shown might seem incredibly low tech, it is worth noting that it represented an important advancement. With this design, firefighters no longer had to run alongside the wagons, but could hop on small running boards for a ride.

This allowed them to conserve their energy for the task at hand. However, the extra weight did tend to exhaust the horses more quickly.

COLUMBIA, SOUTH CAROLINA

With its classical columns and double-porch design, the J.W. Strickland residence in downtown Columbia fits into one of several categories of "Antebellum" (or "plantation") style architecture. Plantations are essentially farms that produce a single crop like lumber, coffee, rubber, or cotton. In the U.S. the word is inextricably bound with African slave labor.

Mr. Strickland was born during the Civil War and operated a livery and stable not far from his residence. At one time, single-family residences primarily populated most American downtowns, an arrangement that would be financially impossible today.

CHICAGO

The Palmer House Hotel, built by developer Potter Palmer and completed in 1925, is a venerable institution known for its opulent design and refined hospitality services. But before there was this Palmer House, there were two earlier versions close to the same spot. Palmer Industries had made its fortune by focusing on customer-friendly retail on State Street.

Next to the first Palmer House in 1871, was a handsome, modest, New England style home typical of the tastes of middle-class Northeasterners who had moved to Chicago. It provides a strikingly unadorned look when compared to today's hotel.

On October 9, 1871, just thirteen days after Palmer House opened, it was unexpectedly destroyed by The Great Chicago Fire along with this residence.

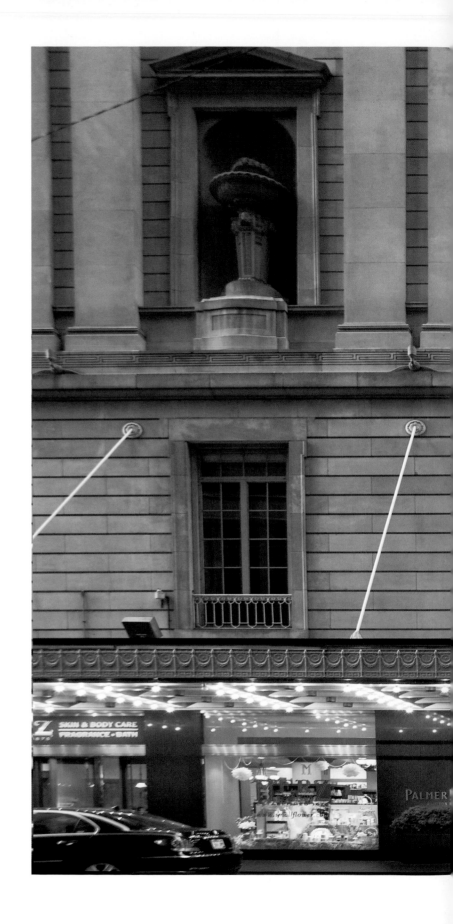

PHOENIX

Outspoken Modernist architect Alfred Beadle has left a prodigious body of work in the Phoenix area. He designed more than eighty commercial structures and eighty residences; many are still standing. One that is not is the Mountain Bell telephone building constructed in the early 1970s, a short way from downtown.

Asbestos issues, combined with the maintenance problems of multiple owners, and a desire to make money in the hot housing market before the crash, all contributed to the demise of what they called "Mo Bell".

The building became (or was allowed to become) an eyesore and was demolished by implosion in 2009. Though he died in 1998, it is thought that Beadles would have supported the demolition because he believed that, once his work was in a distressed condition, it should not continue to exist.

BUFFALO

Beginning in 1804, with its layout of streets radiating like spokes from a wheel, Buffalo took design seriously. Nationally known architects such as Burnham, Richardson, Sullivan, and Wright contributed to the built environment during the economic boom following the opening of the Erie Canal. The elaborate Erie County Saving Bank (1893), designed by George Post, was constructed when Buffalo was the eighth largest city in the nation.

This downtown landmark served the community until 1968, when it was replaced by an office and shopping mall complex, which blocked one of the original radial streets.

TAMPA

Until the late 1800s, most buildings were low-rise like the Knights of Pythias Castle Hall. (The Knights of Pythias were a fraternal organization and secret society.) Beginning with the "Chicago School", buildings were constructed using strong skeleton frames and no longer relied on the outside walls to bear the weight of the structure.

During the 20th century improvements in steel, reinforced concrete, glass, and aluminum—combined with new construction techniques—further advanced the development of high rise towers. And finally, fast elevators and air conditioning addressed issues of user comfort.

DENVER

The original Denver Club, constructed in 1888, was inspired by the nationally influential style of Boston architect H.H. Richardson. Called "Richardsonian Romanesque", these buildings were solid, squat, stone structures with rounded arches and often-decorative horizontal bands. (Behind the club is the faint image of the First Congregational Church — demolished for a theater in 1930). The old Denver Club was torn down in 1954 for Denver's first Modernist high-rise, and relocated to its top floors.

This photograph was taken by William Henry Jackson. Between the 1870s and the early 1900s, he documented the West. His images, along with those of painter Thomas Moran, played a major role in Yellowstone being designated our first National Park.

WILMINGTON, DELAWARE

Wilmington Dry Goods was a classic kind of store that served generations between the 1920s and early 1970s. Perhaps it can best be understood by examining some of its departments: Men's Work Clothes, Shoe Repair, Curtains, Deli, Records, Paints and Hardware, Drugs, Watch Repair, Ladies Hosiery, and Baked Goods.

In terms of variety, it was comparable to one of today's big box department stores. What made it different was the local connection of its owners, and the fact that national chains, with their sophisticated advertising campaigns and foreign suppliers, had not yet come to dominate the market.

HOUSTON

If only one word could be used to describe Houston's Shamrock Hotel, it would be "ambitious". As the largest hotel built nationally in the 1940s, it was ambitious in terms of scale. As a planned convention center several miles from downtown, it was ambitious in terms of location. As a venue for mega-parties, it was ambitious in terms of drawing Hollywood celebrities. With a swimming pool so large that it had waterskiing shows, it was ambitious in terms of generating curiosity. And, finally, with an interior design that featured sixty-three shades of green, (reflecting owner Glenn McCarthy's Irish heritage), it was ambitious in terms of ... green.

Running such an operation was extremely expensive. Despite it being a popular locale for major Houston events, lagging business combined with poor outside investments forced McCarthy to sell the hotel to Hilton Hotels Corporation. The new owners also failed to make it profitable and eventually gave it to the Texas Medical Center, which demolished it for a parking lot in 1987.

CLEVELAND

Late night comedians are not good sources for accurate information about a place. Cleveland has certainly had more than its share of problems. But at one time it was the fifth largest city in the country and a manufacturing powerhouse. During its extended economic downturn, many significant residences were lost; however, important arts and cultural institutions, parks, and architecture survived.

Cleveland is currently busy reinventing itself. The 1900s era commercial area shown here has now become an entertainment destination with an assortment of loft residences close by. It is a reminder about how fluid the life of a city can be.

SAN DIEGO

Across from downtown San Diego is the affluent resort community of Coronado Island. It is probably best known as the location of the Hotel del Coronado, an architectural gem built in 1888.

Several large steamships ferried people—and later cars—to the island. This system functioned relatively well until August 3, 1969, when the sweeping, elegant Coronado Bay Bridge opened for car traffic.

ST. LOUIS

Walking through a large, undeveloped, and untended area of St. Louis surrounded by a chain-link security fence is an eerie urban experience. Over the past forty years this piece of ground has almost completely returned to its natural forested state. But this is not some sort of nature park; rather it is the site of one of the most discussed low-income housing efforts ever.

The massive Pruitt-Igoe housing project that began here with such positive fanfare in 1954, ended in 1972 with the very public implosion of the first of its thirty-three high-rise buildings. (St. Stanislaus Kostka Church, whose spires can be seen in the distance, adjoined the development and still exists).

The colossal failure of Pruitt-Igoe has been explained in terms of design, racism, government regulations, neglect, and culture. Chad Freidrichs' recent documentary *The Pruitt-Igoe Myth* examines these topics in a thought-provoking and intelligent manner.

INDIANAPOLIS

Before the growth of suburban malls, the downtowns of cities were the centers of consumer commerce. Major furniture, appliance and clothing stores were located there. They served not only people who lived in the city, but those who would go "in town" to find the greatest variety, highest quality, or best-priced merchandise.

Vonnegut Hardware on bustling Washington Street was an example of this kind of downtown enterprise. Founded by German immigrants, it operated for a century as a family business.

By some reports, the great grandson of the founder worked here during the summers. But Kurt Vonnegut is much better known as one of the most famous authors and thinkers of the late 20th Century, whose works include *Slaughterhouse Five* and *Breakfast of Champions*.

MEMPHIS

The "Merchant Prince of Memphis", Napoleon Hill, initially made profits by joining the California Gold Rush in his teens, around 1850. After that, one could say everything he touched turned to gold; he profited from a dry goods store opened on the eve of the Civil War, and he invested in banking, real estate, and industrial development in the post-war era. Eventually Hill became the head of a huge cotton processing and storage-system company. He also participated financially in a streetcar line and the Alabama steel industry.

The block where his French Gothic style residence stood from 1881 until 1930 is perhaps just as interesting for what replaced it. In 1930 the tallest office building in the South, the Sterick Building, opened on this site. Highly detailed inside and out, with granite and limestone in the lobby and a green tile roof, it enjoyed a short period of occupation by major tenants. Poor attempts at modernization are thought to have hurt its business, and since the mid 1980s it has remained empty. Although listed on the National Register of Historic Places, it is not protected from demolition.

PITTSBURGH

With a downtown defined by rivers, Pittsburgh is known as the "City of Bridges". Constructed in 1915, the stone and steel North Side Point Bridge crossed the Allegheny River just before it joins with the Monongahela River to form the Ohio River (seen in the background). It carried automobile and streetcar traffic until it was demolished in 1970 for being functionally outdated.

A small section of the bridge's pier was left on the far shore near Heinz Field. It is now the site of a memorial to a local social reformer who became a national figure in children's television as "Mr. Rogers".

BILOXI

The fury of Hurricane Katrina in 2006 produced 27-foot-high surges of water, destroying this Greek Revival beach house and approximately 90% of the other buildings along the Mississippi Coast. Every single county in Mississippi was declared a disaster area.

OAKLAND

When constructed in 1919, the Pacific Telephone & Telegraph building was only six stories high. Re-working and doubling its height in 1927 created an elegant Chicago style office building design reminiscent of a classic Greek column, with a base on the bottom two floors, a capital on the top two floors, and a long supportive pillar on the floors in between.

BIRMINGHAM

The founders of Birmingham, a large percentage of whom descended from England, decided to use the name of an industrial center in their ancestral homeland. And like its namesake, Birmingham became one of the largest iron producers in the country. The Woodward Iron Company benefited from the mineral deposits in the area and business development that stressed "vertical integration"— controlling all aspects of production from mining to transportation.

There are no vestiges of the furnace that used to be located here, but close-by abandoned rails, buildings, and other detritus show evidence of what was once a thriving industry. The company closed in the 1970s due to foreign competition.

LEXINGTON

The Kentucky Association, the oldest turf organization in the country, was formed in 1826 to promote thoroughbred horse racing. One of its undertakings was the construction of a racetrack nicknamed "Chittlin' Switch". To this day, half a dozen races that began here still continue, including "The Phoenix Stakes", the oldest stakes race in the country.

After several changes in ownership, economic problems, and a fire that burned down eighteen neighborhood residences, the track was closed in 1933.

Today the area adjoins a residential neighborhood.

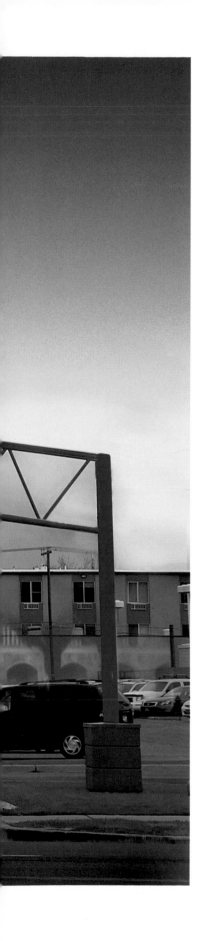

SALT LAKE CITY

Influenced by the 1893 Chicago World's Fair but envisioned as a permanent installation, the Salt Palace and surrounding park were designed by Richard K.A. Kletting. His work on the Utah State Capitol and the Saltair Pavilion had made him the most prominent architect in the state.

A clever and appropriate design element was the use of salt crystals in some of the exterior paint, which added sparkle under daylight or evening lighting.

The pavilion was the heart of the project, and when it burned in 1910, the various amusement park features that adjoined it eventually went out of business.

Today, the location is a car dealership.

CHARLESTON, WEST VIRGINIA

The current "food truck" phenomenon has something in common with the classic diners of one or two generations ago. Diners developed from the horse-drawn "night lunch wagons" of the late 1800s that provided snack options at a time when most restaurants closed by 8pm. Later, refinements such as a counters and stools were added, and "wagons" turned into "diners". The streamlined, train-inspired look began in the 1930s.

The Young brothers opened the Quarrier Diner in 1932 and, following an expansion and remodeling with a second diner, renamed it The Twin Diner in 1936. Following WWII, the family moved The Twin Diner to a new location and replaced it with a larger, more elaborate Art Deco style building. Unfortunately, the menu changes did not appeal to many of their traditional customers. The restaurant has gone though several incarnations and is currently open under different ownership.

WASHINGTON, D.C.

The story of the Belasco Theatre is one of continuous change. Built in 1895, it was originally known as the Lafayette Square Opera House. In 1906 it was bought by a successful New York theater promoter named Belasco; in 1935 it was remodeled into a movie theater; in 1937 it was changed back into a live theater; in 1942 it was owned by the federal government and made into a canteen for entertaining servicemen; and in the 1950s it became a USO club for Korean War servicemen.

In 1964 it was demolished as part of a new master plan for Lafayette Square.

SEATTLE

It is hard to overstate the impact of Andrew Carnegie on libraries around the U.S. and the world. Between 1883 and 1929 nearly 1,700 libraries were built in the U.S. through his partnership with communities both large and small. That was nearly one half of all libraries in the country. The Carnegie libraries were designed in several styles tied to classical movements like Italian Renaissance, Spanish Colonial, and Baroque.

A Carnegie Library in Seattle was built in 1907 between 4th and 5th Streets. Many institutions that own land have a tendency to tear down one building that no longer seems functional and put up a new one on the same spot. This is what happened in 1960 when the Carnegie Library was replaced with a Modernist style library, which was then replaced with a new design by Rem Koolhaas in 2004.

OMAHA

When this photo was taken in 1879, Omaha was about to become one of the fastest growing cities in the country, primarily because of the meat packing industry. The variety of items advertised at this general store reveal a lot about the era, especially the term "druggist".

Nostalgia for the western frontier of the nineteenth century might fade if the state of medicine at that time were to be considered. It is easy to forget that before the twentieth century cures were rarely based on science, but on untested home remedies, doctors who did not understand germ theory, and charlatans who would claim their potions and elixirs were medicinal.

But people wanted cures for their diseases, so they would turn to whatever sounded reasonable or seemed to work. Druggists were common in every community and carried all the herbs, pills, and liquids people desired (or were encouraged to desire). Many contained morphine, opium, cocaine, or alcohol.

CHARLOTTE

At one time, Charlotte's third City Hall stood on this spot. Today it would be in the middle of the Blumenthal Performing Arts Center, the Bank of America Stadium and Hearst Tower.

Public buildings inevitably become too small for the needs of a growing city and are often viewed as out-of-date. And so they are demolished, as this was in 1925.

Interestingly, the next City Hall was protected as an historic landmark and is being used for limited city services.

ST. LOUIS

The St. Louis World's Fair of 1904 (technically the Louisiana Purchase Exposition) was the largest world's fair in U.S. history.

Held at today's Forest Park and the campus of Washington University, it featured over 1,500 buildings. They were constructed with a temporary material called "staff", a mixture of plaster of Paris and hemp. The Saint Louis Art Museum was the only permanent structure from this world's fair.

In addition to the grandeur created by architects like Emmanuel Masqueray and Cass Gilbert, as well as landscaper George Kessler, there were a variety of items first presented or popularized at the event, such as ice cream cones, Dr Pepper, hot dogs, and cotton candy.

Electric typewriters, fax machines, and X-rays were also introduced. And public figures as varied as Helen Keller, Geronimo, and Scott Joplin participated.

Today Forest Park is an expansive multi-use environment that contains museums, athletic fields, and large areas carefully landscaped with trees and water features.

ATLANTA

The story of The Frances Hotel has a melodramatic, theatrical feel. It was "born into wealth and privilege" and "died without a penny to its name".

It was originally built in 1898 as The Ferlinger, Atlanta's first apartment building—a multi-use facility with living units above a high-end grocery store. One of the grocery's amenities was a ladies reception room with a grand piano for 'cultured amusement' while employees gathered items.

The Ferlinger also included a restaurant and rooftop garden that was very popular among Atlanta's financial elite.

Times change, neighborhoods change, and buildings change. In later years The Ferlinger became The Frances Hotel, the wealthy left for more northern areas of the city, and dive bars and strip joints became common in the neighborhood. Eventually The Frances became an important refuge for those one step away from homelessness, with the vestiges of its past apparent only in worn architectural details.

It was demolished in 1985 and is now a vest pocket park.

MILWAUKEE

The Queen Anne Style Industrial Exposition Building was originally built on a swamp in 1878 for the reason expressed in its name. But it was incredibly multi-purposed and the site of a bicycle racetrack, conventions, the Milwaukee Public Museum repository, a skating rink, sporting competitions, concerts, Mardi Gras festivals and funerals.

Burning magnesium from a photographer's flash is suspected in the fire that destroyed the Exposition Building in 1905. An auditorium replaced it and is now part of a new theater complex.

PROVIDENCE

When photographed in 1958 for the Historic American Building Survey, this structure was described simply as "an example of early commercial buildings along the Providence waterfront". It was titled "James Brown Warehouse".

Brown is probably the most famous name in Providence, primarily because the family included the wealthy benefactors who founded Brown University, the prestigious Ivy League school. John Brown (James' father) and his three brothers had amassed a fortune in the fields of manufacture and trade. They produced candles and pig iron and sailed goods to the West Indies. And, most significantly, they participated in the slave trade. This relatively recent revelation, and the dramatic, complex story of how John's brother Moses split with him to become an activist for abolition can only be introduced here.

KANSAS CITY, MISSOURI

Certainly the most famous alumnus of the *Kansas City Star* newspaper is the novelist Ernest Hemingway, whose spare style stemmed directly from his journalism days.

The *Kansas City Star* began publishing in 1880, four years before Harry Truman was born. Ultimately, it would a take a rather critical stance about the thirty-third President of the U.S. Seeing a street sign with his name in front of the *Star*'s gleaming new building would, no doubt, have pleased Truman.

The *Star*'s bold design stands in strong contrast to the commercial buildings of 1917. Eventually more and more of these buildings became car dealerships as auto manufacturers chose this area for their showrooms.

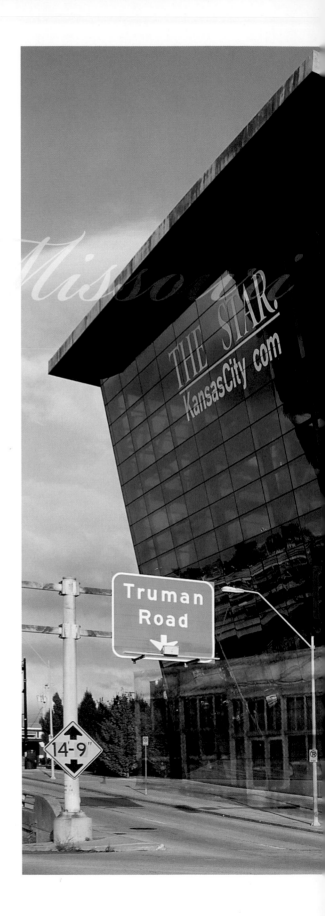

BUFFALO

In 1825, the 363-mile Erie Canal opened, connecting the Hudson River in Albany with Lake Erie in Buffalo. Soon Buffalo became a major railroad, steel, and grain-milling center. The grain elevator was actually invented in Buffalo; it provided a way to store grain and trade in bulk rather than small sacks.

The Dakota grain elevator, shown here, was built in 1901 and demolished in 1965. It was constructed of steel and iron, a departure from earlier structures that were wooden and highly fire prone.

PHILADELPHIA

The Broad Street Theater, with its Moorish style inside and out, opened under the more exotic name of Kiralfy's Alhambra Palace in 1876. It was the site of major theatrical spectacles and provided amenities like a restaurant and beer garden.

By 1937 the theater had lost much of its appeal, as well as its original architecture, and was demolished.

Broad Street today is known as the "Avenue of the Arts". It includes numerous institutions, such as The Philadelphia Orchestra and the Pennsylvania Academy of Fine Arts, America's oldest art school.

CLEVELAND

During the early part of the twentieth century, up until The Great Depression, "interurban" passenger traffic was particularly active between ports in the Great Lakes. There were even special honeymoon deals to Buffalo and Niagara Falls.

The 9th Street Pier was a lively center of arrivals, departures, taxi traffic, and connections to railroads. After WWII business severely diminished and new uses for waterfronts were considered. Some cities chose to develop these areas as parkland. Others, like Cleveland, refashioned them as entertainment centers with museums, sports venues, and restaurants.

The most notable institution now sitting by 9th street is The Rock and Roll Hall of Fame, a set of white geometric forms designed by I.M. Pei. Clevelanders lobbied hard to get this institution, pointing out that in the early 1950s famed local disc jockey, Alan Freed, helped popularize this new musical genre and the term "rock and roll".

NEW ORLEANS

One of New Orleans' multiple music traditions is opera. In fact, it was the first American city to support an opera. The passion of many nineteenth century residents for this dramatic art form matches that of today's sports fans.

The French Opera House graced the corner of Toulouse and Bourbon Streets between the Civil War and WWI. It was the venue for numerous American premieres by European composers, as well as the site of balls, receptions, and fundraisers.

Designed by James Gallier Jr, this Greek Revival style building was destroyed by fire in 1919. A hotel is now located on its site, and acknowledges the past by sponsoring free performances with the New Orleans Opera Association.

FORT WORTH

The story of the Landmark Tower office building is one of extreme highs and lows. Completed in 1957, it was the tallest building in town. In 2006, it was the tallest building in Texas ever to be imploded.

In between, it was the victim of economic downturns, the locale of a bold plan to become residences, the target of a major tornado, and the neglected child of an owner who wanted to turn it into a parking lot.

PHOENIX

The Q & Q Malt Shop served the culinary needs of Baby Boomers at Phoenix Union High School. Today it would have an ideal setting—an entrance to Arizona State University's downtown campus.

RICHMOND, VIRGINIA

Monument Avenue, lined with trees and stately residences, seems to have one foot in the present and one in the past. The number and frequency of joggers feels very contemporary, while the nature of the monuments—all Confederate Civil War heroes except for tennis great Arthur Ashe—is a strong connection to the past. Not surprisingly, the attitudes toward the veneration of these figures divides citizens.

Substantial present day homes can seem quite modest when compared with the enormous residence of Whitmell S. Forbes built in 1914. He owned the entire block, and his house was defined by its elaborate Classical detailing combined with monumentality. The entrance portico was nearly forty feet high. When he lost his wealth in The Great Depression, the house was demolished.

MINNEAPOLIS

On the banks of the Mississippi in 1855, German immigrant Gottlieb Gluek started the first brewery in what would soon be named Minneapolis. He and his sons overcame significant challenges. They had to maintain 110 draft horses to pull their wagons. And they had to rebuild after a devastating fire, for which they were underinsured, by using family funds.

From 1920 to 1933 the brewery weathered Prohibition by making non-alcoholic "near beer" and soft drinks. They kept up with canning technology and created an early "light beer" too. In 1964 the Gluek Brewing Company finally fell to the competition from giant national corporations, as had so many before them.

Two years later, the Gluek's brewery and substantial residence (on right) also fell when the new owners demolished it. Gluek Park now sits on its location.

MILWAUKEE

Perhaps we could call the Goodyear Blimp Reliance an example of airborne architecture. It was a regular fixture at Maitland Field, a small airport on Lake Michigan that opened in 1927. One hundred and forty feet long and filled with helium, its top speed was 60 miles per hour. It could carry only six passengers and was never a practical form of transportation.

Maitland Field generally was not a financial success. In its last days, it became the location of missile silos ready to intercept nuclear weaponized ICBMs (intercontinental ballistic missiles) presumably from the Soviet Union. Fortunately, this scenario never materialized, and in 1970 the facility became the new home of Summerfest, currently billed as the world's largest music festival.

In the foreground are large reflective kinetic sculptures.

MIAMI

It is hard to believe that Miami Beach, currently so enamored and protective of its large collection of Art Deco buildings, had watched them slide into disrepair and demolition up until the 1970s. Also notable is that this amazing collection of hotels and apartments was designed by just a few architects during the 30s, 40s, and 50s.

The Great Depression had made mammoth hotels financially unworkable, and several designers, including Henry Hohauser, stepped forward to create smaller "boutique" hotels. They were influenced by the design style Art Decoratif that debuted in Paris in 1925. It emphasized geometric decoration and a streamlined quality that celebrated the machine age.

The Collins Park Hotel was one of Hohauser's over 200 projects, but in recent years it and several other nearby hotels in the Art Deco Historic District were destroyed, probably by arson. Currently, a bold plan to restore, renovate, and update the entire block is in the works.

ALBUQUERQUE

Celebrated in song, legend, and a hit television show, "Route 66" was at one time the main highway from Chicago to Los Angeles. And it went straight through downtown Albuquerque.

Following WWII, "66" was an especially popular vacation route and spawned an assortment of eye-catching restaurants, motels, and gas stations to lure travelers. The Iceberg Cafe must have been irresistible to anyone who was overheated, had children, or a sense of humor.

The mammoth Interstate Highway System that begun construction in the 1950s and finished in the 1980s, spelled the end for "Route 66". And in 1985 it was actually "decertified" as a highway.

However "The Main Street of America" lives on in places like Albuquerque, where it is now simply Central Avenue. Much is gone, but much of what remains has been repurposed. Gas stations have become restaurants, motels have become offices, and a residence has become a hostel.

CHICAGO

From 1905 to 1961, the Republic (Strong) Building occupied this site. It was a classic example of the "Commercial Style" of architecture later known as the "Chicago School". These were early high-rises that used steel frame construction and had strong vertical lines and subtle, classically inspired decoration.

In 1961, it was demolished and replaced by the Home Federal Building, a new classic, but of the Modernist style, with no ornamentation and a pristine glass and metal exterior.

SAN FRANCISCO

Adolph Sutro, who made a fortune inventing mining technology, served as Mayor of San Francisco and also owned 8% of the city. On the one hand, he had a lavish personal home and gardens with views to the ocean and the bay. On the other, he had a populist streak and a desire to provide amusement for all.

The location of his land on the windy cliffs and dunes of the city did not have quite the appeal that it does today. And the beaches in San Francisco have never been comfortable for swimming. So, in 1896, Sutro created the largest indoor "baths" in the world. Pools of various sizes used seawater and ranged from hot to very chilly. The largest was an impressive 300 by 125 feet. The Sutro Baths had the refined Sutro touch with gardens, a museum, and a gymnasium. And it was affordable to the average citizen.

In 1906 it was badly damaged in the famous earthquake, and though repaired, it lost some of its glamour and, consequently, some of its business. The Sutro Baths held on until 1952. During demolition in the 1960s it burned, leaving stone ruins that are a fascinating part of the Golden Gate National Recreation Area today.

CHARLOTTE

Charlotte's recent economic history has had a profound impact on the built environment, especially along the central avenue of Tryon Street. High-rise office towers, major arts institutions, vest pocket parks, and restored historic structures are all part of the new fabric. Charlotte is now the second largest banking center in the U.S. and has a varied economy connected to energy, communications, and manufacturing.

The striking Bechtler Museum of Modern Art, designed by Mario Botta, replaced a business designed mainly for easy drop off and pick up.

WASHINGTON D.C.

Following the Civil War, many former slaves, often called "freedmen", were impoverished and without access to capital. In 1865, the Lincoln administration supported a Republican congressional proposal for a bank to serve the community of ex-slaves and black veterans. It allowed for individual savings and made funds available to organizations such as schools, hospitals, and churches.

Eventually, there were 18 branches of the Freedman's Savings Bank with a headquarters in D.C. across from the White House. Faced with the consequences of certain business decisions and the economic panic of 1873, even its last president, the dynamic abolitionist Frederick Douglass, could not save it from closing in 1874.

INDIANAPOLIS

What makes a building valuable to a community? And why should some buildings be saved? This is certainly a subject for in-depth analysis. But to start, we could say that a building is a piece of utilitarian art with a function, a form, and a meaning. Using these three elements we could begin to evaluate it.

Numerous buildings have been demolished because they were no longer considered as performing a "function". By the 1950s, The Marion County Courthouse (built in 1877), was overcrowded, untended, and not up to contemporary office standards. This consideration often trumps all others. Here we might ask, "Was an alternative usage for the building examined?".

The "form" of the building was a mixture of classical styles, beautiful to some eyes and dated to others. Many government buildings of the time could be described this way, and the loss of one perhaps seemed of no great significance to some. Here we might ask, "Are we just focused on current tastes, or the future fabric of our city?".

Initially, the "meaning" of a building might seem like an odd concept. But by simply giving an imaginary voice to it we can begin to better understand its meaning. The classical courthouse perhaps originally said: " I am stable, carefully designed and show the value that Indianapolis places on justice".

Meaning can evolve over time. Many now mourn the loss of the Marion County Courthouse, knowing it can never be recovered. Today, the ghost of the building might say, "I represent a shared history that is lost, as well as an elaborate, detailed beauty that is absent from much of our contemporary built environment".

HARTFORD

Hartford has the second oldest secondary school in the country. (Boston Latin School was the first). It began in 1638 as a preparatory school for young men going into Puritan ministries.

It was not until the concept of general academics became popular in the 1800s that the word "high school" came into existence.

In 1883, Hartford built a new high school overlooking the capitol. It was designed by George Keller, who has left a legacy of memorable public buildings in the immediate area.

Hartford High School was demolished for a new east / west highway in the 1960s.

HOUSTON

Controversy surrounded the Moorish style Federal building that once occupied this corner of Fannin and Franklin. Its highly decorated style and misassumptions about desert-like climate conditions in Houston seemed to reflect an ignorance of culture and location by removed designers. It served as a courthouse and post office as well as a customs house, making it the center of diverse immigrant activity.

It was demolished in 1937.

CINCINNATI

The Cincinnati Music Hall is the main venue for the symphony orchestra and a storied place for traveling musicians. In 1878, it was constructed with the added purpose of hosting expositions. In 1880 the Democratic National Convention was held there.

Because it was built on a pauper's cemetery, stories of ghosts abound.

Recognized as a National Historic Landmark in 1977, it has gone through a variety of renovations over the years. The lost bridge pictured here was a temporary connection to Washington Park across the street.

KANSAS CITY, KANSAS

Hare & Hare were a father and son landscape firm established in 1910 in Kansas City, Missouri. The father, Sidney, had learned his craft while working as a cemetery superintendent. The son, Harry, studied at Harvard under the nation's most famous landscape architect, Frederick Law Olmsted (New York's Central Park, Stanford University campus). Together, the Hares worked in twenty-eight states in a variety of styles that respected local geography and history.

One of their projects in Kansas City, Kansas, included a sunken garden with limestone walls, fountains, and a lily pond. This apparently very refined park space was filled in within twenty years because it was difficult to maintain. It is now an unpaved parking lot.

ASHEVILLE, NORTH CAROLINA

Pack Square has been the central gathering area for this North Carolina city since before it was named after philanthropist George Pack in 1900. Celebrations, solemn occasions, and protests have taken place here. But mainly it has been a spot for simple relaxation.

Downtown Asheville is primarily a low-rise, intimate place with numerous stylish, but not overwhelmingly grand buildings. In 1980, an effort to re-energize Pack Square with the addition of a large office building (and consequently, the demolition of a long row of traditional commercial buildings) was very much in line with national trends of the time. Though designed by famed architect I.M. Pei, it seems completely out of scale with the rest of the park and unconnected to its surroundings.

More recently, the park's human amenities were renovated. And the dominant trend in Asheville now is adapting old buildings to new uses.

NEW YORK

Cornelius Vanderbilt II was a grandson of "Commodore" Cornelius Vanderbilt who, during the early to mid 1800s, became the richest man in the U.S., first with his steamship business and then with his railroads. His family legacy of wealth and celebrity includes palatial homes like The Biltmore Estate in Asheville, North Carolina, and The Breakers in Newport, Rhode Island, as well as Vanderbilt University. Painter, fashion designer, and author Gloria Vanderbilt and her son, television journalist Anderson Cooper, are descendants.

The "Commodore" lived modestly, but the degree of ostentatious wealth displayed by his progeny was unprecedented. New York's 5th Avenue, the location of many of their homes, included the largest residence in the city, just below Central Park and across from the Plaza Hotel, owned by Cornelius II. Designed by nationally known architect George Post, it had a staff of thirty-seven.

By 1927 it was financially unsupportable, even by Cornelius II's widow Alice Claypoole Gwynne, and was demolished. Today it is the location of high-end retailer Bergdorf Goodman.

DALLAS

An elaborate newsstand flanked the side of The Oriental Hotel, the city's premier inn, constructed in 1890 and demolished thirty-four years later. The location is now a small pocket park between two downtown streets.

DENVER

Curtis Street, Denver's "Great White Way" of the 1910s and 1920s, was a dazzlingly lit series of movie theaters and vaudeville venues, and the location of the Tabor Opera House. It stretched for about six blocks. Remarkably, Denver had a population of 230,000 at the time, and claimed a 100,000 per day theater attendance rate.

Silent film stars like Charlie Chaplin, Laurel and Hardy, and Tom Mix (who was featured as a cowboy in many early Westerns) would visit periodically to perform live. Thomas Edison was also very complimentary about the street, which undoubtedly used thousands of his bulbs.

The U.S. entrance into WWII, and social changes afterward, ultimately doomed every theater on this street. Today the general area is a burgeoning live theater district, but Curtis Street has missed out on any of the current glitz.

CHARLESTON

All that remains of the Thompson Auditorium in Cannon Park are four Corinthian columns. But they stand as a dramatic sculptural reminder of the past. Originally built in 1899 for a reunion of Confederate soldiers, the building later served as a theater and a hospital before becoming an art museum— one of the very oldest in the country. It burned in 1980. Today the area is a park especially popular with dog owners.

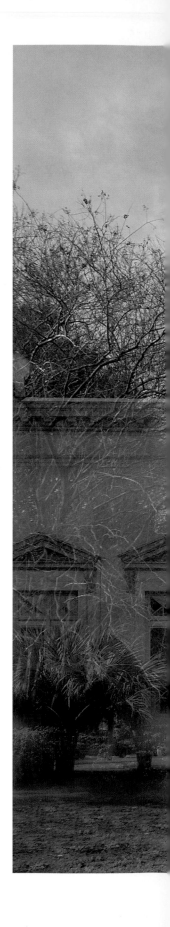

NASHVILLE

Between 1880 and 1900 there were ten World's Fairs—and that was just in the U.S. The 1897 Tennessee Centennial and International Exposition was held in Nashville, with Memphis and Nashville each having a major presence.

Memphis, named for the ancient capital of Egypt, was represented by a pyramid. Unlike the real pyramids, it was made of plaster and is long gone.Nashville, known as the "Athens of the South", was represented by a replica of the Parthenon. The latter was originally planned as a temporary structure, but the city decided to rebuild it with permanent materials. It remains today in Centennial Park and contains a monumental statue of Athena.

COLUMBUS, OHIO

Buildings can resonate in a myriad of ways with different viewers. To some, the Christopher Inn (1867–1988) was a high profile place to work, attend a bar mitzvah, or catch the lounge act of house musician Bob Allen.

To others it was an example of mid-century Modernism that was demolished just before its style gained popularity with preservationists.

And, finally, to some it was most notable for having been designed by a person from a highly under-represented group in the world of architecture. It was created by African-American architect Leon Ransom who, during his short life (1939–1971) designed a significant number of commercial, public, and religious projects in Columbus.

SAVANNAH

Savannah has a unique layout with some twenty mossy parks / squares. Surrounding these are buildings, primarily residences, from various periods since the city's establishment in 1733. (Savannah's current attention to preservation does not go back nearly that far). Today Savannah is a leader in the "adaptive reuse" of its older architecture. Savannah College of Art and Design has created a campus from some sixty existing buildings.

Like so many other U.S. cities, Savannah, in the not-too-distant past, made decisions that today would be unthinkable. The prospect of profit, the appeal of convenience, and the lack of value placed on the past are why a spectacular and cleverly designed building like Union Station was demolished and replaced by a highway bridge.

LAS VEGAS

Competition for tourists seeking out new experiences has made the Las Vegas Strip the most constantly reinvented "neighborhood" in the U.S. The Landmark Hotel, just off the Strip, had a distinctive tower and unique meandering swimming pool when it opened in 1969. Liberace headlined here. And at one time, Howard Hughes—the eccentric aviator, inventor, movie producer, developer, billionaire, and recluse—was its owner.

However, The Landmark was plagued by construction difficulties, debt, corruption, and the most serious of problems: losing its trendiness. It was imploded in 1995 having spent much of its life empty.

ATLANTIC CITY

This small city has fostered many large plans, schemes, and dreams.

From its beginnings as a health resort with huge hotels and its heyday serving liquor during Prohibition, to its dramatic slide into disrepair after WWII and its reinvention as a gambling destination in the 1970s, Atlantic City has had its share of high profile players.

One such character was Captain John Young, who made his money in amusement parks and built a unique offshore Italian-style marble villa on his "Million Dollar Pier" in 1908. It included a formal sculpture garden, and lighting designed by his close friend, Thomas Edison.

GALVESTON

The Ursuline Academy (completed in 1847 and demolished in 1961) was a Victorian Gothic building that towered over the one-story school that replaced it. Operated by Catholic nuns, but for girls of all faiths, the academy provided refuge for 1,000 residents during the hurricane of 1900, the most deadly in American history.

Damaged by Hurricane Carla in 1961, it was demolished when it probably could have been repaired.

Q & A WITH T. JOHN HUGHES

What are some of your influences for *Apparitions*?

Well, first of all, I'd say my years as a commercial architectural photographer and a college instructor where I also specialized in photo history. I have long been drawn to buildings and the nature of urban environments, particularly how they have been captured in photographs since the early 1800s. Also, certain movies about change over time really resonate for me, such as Michael Apted's ambitious documentary of children every seven years to adulthood and Wayne Wang's *Smoke* in which the lead character takes a photo of the front of his shop every day.

Finally, I should say I am an appreciator of all manner of before-and-after imagery, and I mean *all* manner, "from the sublime to the ridiculous"—from overlays showing how Roman ruins originally looked, to then-and-now books about cities, to shots of celebrities before and after plastic surgery.

Have you done any other photography yourself with a before-and-after theme?

Yes, the Cityscape Panorama Project (cityscapepanorama. com) is an every-five-year documentation of downtown Denver that I began in 1992. Using a panoramic camera, I shoot forty cityscapes and streetscapes under similar lighting conditions. I have had numerous shows of this work along the way, and my goal is to arrange for it to be continued into the indefinite future.

How did *Apparitions* then start to take shape?

Slowly. Keep in mind that my first thoughts were during the pre-digital years where the logistical problems of combining images were way beyond my reach. But newer and better technology developed, and I became more digitally savvy thanks to my "byte head" colleagues at The Art Institute of Colorado. Then I enrolled in an online Master's program in digital photography through Savannah College of Art and Design (also courtesy of the Institute). I finally had an opportunity to try to manifest my idea with a few buildings in Denver.

Soon afterward, I was taking a road trip and decided to try shooting in other cities. And the next thing you know, I was traveling just to shoot. Eventually I visited every region of the continental U.S. It took about six years, with three of them heavily devoted to the project. I like to say that I took a modestly lucrative vocation of photography and turned it into a highly expensive avocation.

How do you choose your buildings?

In general, I want a wide spectrum of subjects. They are not uniformly architectural gems—although that "species" is well represented. So they are public buildings, commercial buildings, and residences, combined with sites of temporary events, socially significant spots, and offbeat Americana.

Before I go to a city, I do some informal research. There are hundreds of books like *Lost Chicago* by David Lowe or *San Diego Then and Now* by Nancy Hendrickson or *Historic Photos of Memphis* by Cordell and O'Daniel.

I look at interesting materials online created by individuals or institutions, like "Tampa Changing" by Bryan Weinstein. And sometimes I might call an organization like the San Antonio Conservation Society (founded way back in 1924) for advice. Additionally, I examine some locations on the amazing Google Earth.

I make extensive use of the Library of Congress and the Historic American Building Survey (HABS), which began in the 1930s and, in my view, is a national treasure.

So you have many resources to examine, but how do you make final choices about your subjects?

Wait a minute; I'm not quite finished with resources. If you'll notice, this book is dedicated to librarians everywhere. When I get to a city, my first stop is typically the special collections at the central library. This is where I am introduced to various other sources and suggestions. The helpful and often enthusiastic staffs of these places have really been my allies in *Apparitions*. And not one has ever told me to "shhh".

So I take all the information I've examined, determine if the historical images are available and typically select four or five locations that intrigue me.

When it finally comes down to choosing what images to have in the book, I focus on quality and variety. Sometimes I have included two images from one city and none from another. Here's an analogy: When a sports team is drafting new players you will often hear them say they are looking for someone to fill a certain position, but if a special athlete is available they will choose them, whatever the position. I will often choose a very strong shot over a weaker one that is simply from a city I want to include.

153

Do you want your images to be emblematic of the cities where you shoot?

Sometimes they are, but many times they aren't. A high rise in New York or a casino in Las Vegas are defining elements of those places; but a hotel does not represent Columbus and a residence does not symbolize Columbia.

You've said that *Apparitions* calls on you to be an "urban detective". How so?

The detective work comes in as I search to find the right spot where earlier projects existed. It can be both frustrating and exhilarating. Streets change, people's memories are not always accurate, historical maps conflict and whole areas can be completely transformed. And so when I find a distant hill, an almost hidden roof, or some other clue that orients an older image to the current setting, I experience one of the most satisfying aspects of the whole process.

Now, sometimes local citizens can be extremely helpful. For example, I was in Galveston and needed to figure out exactly where the cathedral-like Ursuline Academy had been situated. Staff at the new academy suggested that I speak to a woman in her eighties who had attended the older academy and worked at the new academy, but had left for the day.

I gave her a call. She offered to drive back to the academy right then and proceeded not only to answer my question, but to give me a wonderful historic tour of the institution. It was truly a rich experience. I thanked her profusely when she was leaving, though she brushed off my compliments saying, "Once an Ursuline, always an Ursuline".

And speaking of helpful people, sometimes I get help I don't really need. I had an experience in Albuquerque that puts a smile on my face. One Christmas Day I was scouting locations, and at one point I was standing in an empty lot with a bag slung over my shoulder, bundled up, wearing a knit cap, reading some notes. A van pulled up and a friendly lady got out, came over and handed me a package of treats and grooming items. Apparently she thought I was homeless—and can you blame her? Everyone else in the area was homeless, and they all looked just like me!

So what are the next steps?

Bear in mind that research and shooting are like gathering the raw materials of the project. When I combine old and new through Photoshop, I really see what is working. This can be the most time consuming part of the whole process as I seek to create "readable" images.

The last pieces of the project are the explanatory texts that are intended to complement the photo composites. Here I draw on varied topics from architecture, preservation, history, politics, social trends, and popular culture.

Apparitions is obviously about change over time. What else do you want to communicate?

If I can step into my educator's role for a moment, I might point out that many observers believe all photographs are in some manner about time. Images such as Harold Edgerton's one millionth of a second view of a speeding bullet or Michael Wesley's two-year-long exposure of city development seem to wear time on their sleeves. More subtly, our family portraits show a person frozen in time that will affect us differently as their life story unfolds.

Apparitions obviously has time as one of its major themes. I hope the images will also help generate a discussion about the preservation of buildings and culture. I also might mention what I call "the preservation of memory". How often have you looked at a location and tried to remember what was there, even recently, before the latest building? It is often quite difficult. Photos are keys to memories, and the taste of a memory can be so redolent of a time, you want to hold on to it.

Do you have favorite cities?

Those that surprise me, which is a very long list. It is notable how many of us carry dated images of places. I think our perceptions come partly from television sitcoms or news reports, or simplistic political pigeonholing. Clichés are easy and lazy ways of "knowing" things.

Nowadays I tend to go to a city with fewer preconceptions. Each visit is a little adventure.

I have a soft spot for what I call the "incredible shrinking cities", places like Buffalo, Cleveland, St. Louis and Detroit that have lost a lot of their population. These cities were once industrial powerhouses and are now going through long transitions to a changed economy. Each has a wealth of architecture, parks, and institutions from those glory days, and it is inspiring to observe their current efforts to reinvent themselves. I hope that each builds its future while retaining what makes it unique.

Well, finally, is there a future for *Apparitions* past this book?

At first I thought that it had essentially reached a point of completion, but I plan to continue at a reduced pace, just because I enjoy it so damn much.

PHOTOGRAPHER CREDITS

ACKNOWLEDGMENTS

Angela Faris-Belt, Chris Meyer, Georgia Burleson, Gerald Pryor, Liz Schnaitter, Mark Sink, National Trust for Historic Preservation, Patti Barry-Levi, Paul Weinrauch, Rosemary DeMartini, Savannah College of Art and Design, The Art Institute of Colorado, Trinity College (CT), Walter Powers, Paul Latham, Gina Tsarouhas, Ryan Marshall, Rod Gilbert and Sabita Naheswaran from The Images Publishing Group.

And

Bets, Richard H, Brad, Joe, Dave, George M, Pom Pom Dana, Joey P, Beth N, Bob S, Scot, John F, Jamie and Sister Liz, Lisa Gedgaudas, Big Mac and Laura, M'Nerves, Janice M, Steve and Patricia, Dan and Sharon, Charlie H, Cousin Barb and Ben, Randy and Deana, Jerry and Heather, Joan and Ralph, Lloyd, Lynn, Zelma, Terry H, Paramus Lori and family, Johnny Diamond and Robin, Travelin' Chase, Baltimore Bill, Stan the Hurricane Man, Cousin Marge and Tim, Merna, Paulina and Bruce, Ricki and family, George F, Dan, Tom and Tamara, Emil and Marion, Walter the Muse and Dianne, Peter and Elaine, Charlene, Suze and Jay, Mom, Dad, and Jim.